Note to Parents and Teachers

The READING ABOUT: STARTERS series introduces key science vocabulary to young children while encouraging them to discover and understand the world around them. The series works as a set of graded readers in three levels.

LEVEL 2: BEGIN TO READ ALONE follows guidelines set out in the National Curriculum for Year 2 in schools. These books can be read alone or as part of guided or group reading. Each book has three sections:

• Information pages that introduce key words. These key words appear in bold for easy recognition on pages where the related science concepts are explained.
• A lively story that recalls this vocabulary and encourages children to use these words when they talk and write.
• A quiz and index ask children to look back and recall what they have read.

Questions for Further Investigation

SWITCH IT ON explains key concepts about USING ELECTRICITY. Here are some suggestions for further discussion linked to the questions on the information spreads:

p. 5 *Do you know where trains get their electricity from?* Ask children to look at picture – train gets electricity from wires. Electricity flows along wires from a power station.

p. 7 *Why are electric wires put up in the air or underground?* Electricity is very dangerous so most wires are put where people cannot easily touch them.

p. 9 *What happens if this woman pulls out the plug again?* Reinforce the idea that electricity can only flow to the machine when it is connected, e.g. by a wire or lead.

p. 11 *What do electric machines do in your home?* Ask children to make a list, grouping machines by room or by what they do, e.g. light, sound, computers, moving machines.

p. 13 *Why are there few switches or sockets in a bathroom?* Explain that electricity flows easily in water, so it is easy to get a shock in a bathroom if you are wet from washing. That's why bathroom lights are often turned on with a long cord not a switch.

p. 15 *Why are batteries different sizes?* Some jobs need more energy. A watch doesn't need much energy, so a small battery will do. A torch needs more energy – and bigger batteries.

p. 19 *Can you guess what happens when electric wires are damaged in a storm?* Explain that blown over poles/cut wires can create a break in the circuit, causing a power cut.

p. 21 *Why do you think a bus or space shuttle can't use a lead?* How long would they be?

p. 23 *Where in the world would solar panels work best?* Sunny places! And wind farms?

ADVISORY TEAM

Educational Consultant
Andrea Bright – Science Co-ordinator, Trafalgar Junior School, Twickenham

Literacy Consultant
Jackie Holderness – former Senior Lecturer in Primary Education, Westminster Institute, Oxford Brookes University

Series Consultants
Anne Fussell – Early Years Teacher and University Tutor, Westminster Institute, Oxford Brookes University

David Fussell – C.Chem., FRSC

CONTENTS

4   electricity, energy, machine

6   flow, wire, pylon

8   switch, socket, plug, lead

10   light, sound, heat

12   mains, shock, safe

14   battery, positive, negative

16   circuit, bulb, holder

18   connect, break

20   motor, cell

22   power station, turbine, lightning

24   **Story: Power Cut!**
What do Luke and Hugh do
when the electricity gets cut off?

31   Quiz

32   Index

PAPERBACK EDITION PRINTED 2007

© Aladdin Books Ltd 2005

Designed and produced by
Aladdin Books Ltd
2/3 Fitzroy Mews
London W1T 6DF

First published in 2005
in Great Britain by
Franklin Watts
338 Euston Road
London NW1 3BH

Franklin Watts Australia
Hachette Children's Books
Level 17/207 Kent Street
Sydney NSW 2000

A catalogue record for this
book is available from the
British Library.
Dewey Classification: 537
ISBN 978 07496 7525 7

Printed in Malaysia

All rights reserved

Editor: Sally Hewitt

Design: Flick, Book Design
and Graphics

Thanks to: The pupils of Trafalgar
Infants School, Twickenham • Luke, Hugh
and Sara Pullman • Lynne Thompson •
The pupils and teachers of Trafalgar
Junior School, Twickenham and St.
Nicholas C.E. Infant School, Wallingford.

Photocredits:

l-left, r-right, b-bottom, t-top,
c-centre, m-middle
Cover tl & tr, 3, 9tr, 10tr, 13tr,
14ml, 16 all, 18tr, 19, 20, 24 both,
26 all, 27mr, 27bl, 28 both, 29,
30tl, 31br, 31bc — Jim Pipe. Cover
b, 2tl, 2bl, 5br, 8, 10b, 13b, 14mr,
14br, 15 all, 17 both, 18b, 22m, 31bl
— Marc Arundale/Select Pictures.
2ml, 5m, 30tr — Corel. 4tr, 14tr,
25mr, 25bl, 27tl, 31ml — Corbis.
4b, 11m, 23 both — Photodisc. 6tr
— Comstock. Cover tm, 6b, 22tr,
22bl — European Community. 7tr
— Brand X Pictures. 7b — PBD. 9b
— Flick Smith. 11br, 14bl, 32 —
Ingram Publishing. 21tl — Ballard
Bus Program. 21b — NASA. 25tr
— Hugh Pullman.

USING
ELECTRICITY

Switch It On

By Jim Pipe

Aladdin/Watts
London • Sydney

Everything needs **energy** to work and to move.

Cars and trucks get **energy** from fuel.

Electric **machines** get **energy** from **electricity**.

You get your energy from food and drinks.

Fuel

Electric **machines** can be small, like an alarm clock, or big, like a train.

Powerful trains need a lot of **energy**. They use a lot of **electricity**.

Train

A CD player only needs a little **electricity**.

• Do you know where trains get their electricity from?

Electricity comes from a power plant.
It **flows** along **wires** into our homes.

Tall poles and **pylons** carry
the **wires** up in the air.
Can you see any **wires**
outside your house?

Pylons

Never fly a kite
where there
are electric
wires in the air.

6

Wires carry electricity around your home.

Most of these **wires** are under the ground or in the walls of your house.

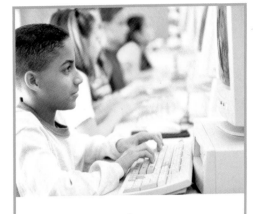

We use electricity at home, at school, and at work.

Electricity **flows** all day and night. You can turn on a light or TV at any time.

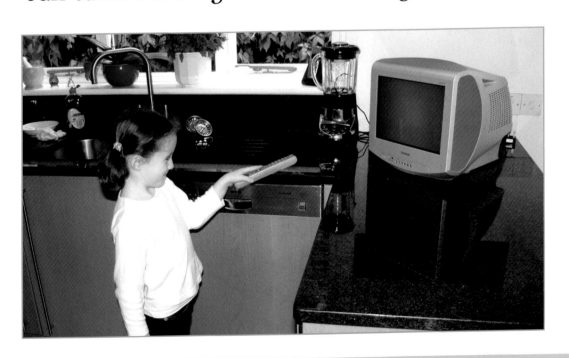

• Why are electric wires put up in the air or underground?

Wires in the walls carry electricity from **switches** to lights.

You press a **switch** one way to turn a light on. You press it the other way to turn a light off.

Switch

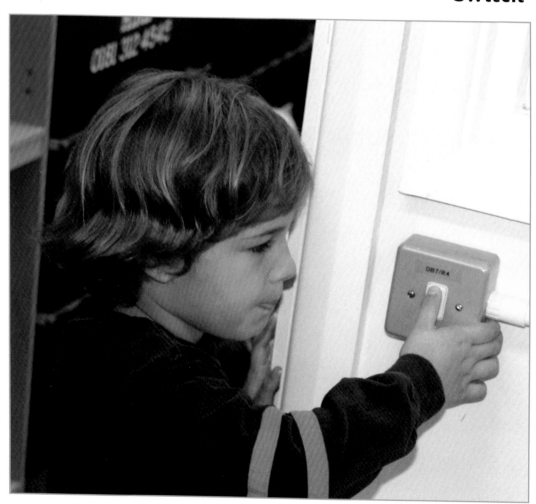

Wires also carry electricity to **outlets**.
We **plug** machines into **outlets** to
make them work.

Electricity flows from
the **electricity** along
the **lead**. This is a wire
that goes to the
machine.

Plugging in

Always ask an adult
to plug an electric
machine in for you.

• What happens if this woman pulls out the plug again?

Electricity is very useful.
Machines use electricity to
do many different things.

Lamps give off **light**.
Radios and televisions
make **sound** and pictures.

Ovens and hair dryers **heat** things up.
Refrigerators and freezers make them cold.

**Hair
dryer**

Look around your house. What machines must you plug in?

Computer

Some machines like flashlights use electricity but don't need to be plugged in.

Simple machines like staplers and scissors don't need electricity at all.

Stapler

• What do electric machines do in your home?

Electricity from an outlet is called **mains** electricity. It is very dangerous. If **mains** electricity flowed into you it would give you a nasty **shock**. It could even kill you.

Danger!
Electricity

BE SAFE: this sign tells you to watch out for electricity.

Always use electric machines **safely**:

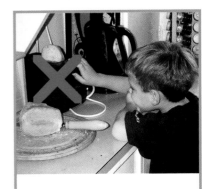

- Never play with machines that plug in.
- Never touch anything electric with wet hands.
- Ask an adult to plug machines in for you.

Machines like toasters can get very hot. So don't touch!

- Keep electric objects away from babies.

Some electric machines use **batteries**. A **battery** stores electricity. When this is used up, we say the **battery** has run out.

Bigger **batteries** store more energy. Can you guess the right **battery** for these machines?

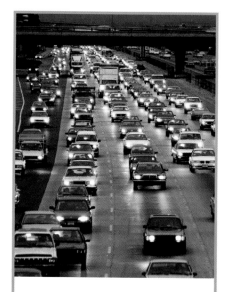

Cars use big batteries to start their engine and to shine their lights.

Watch

Batteries

Flashlight

14

If you look at a **battery**, see if you can find the signs ✚ and ▬.

✚ shows the **positive** end of a battery.
▬ shows the **negative** end of a battery.

The **battery** must be the right way around for a machine to work.

• Why are batteries different sizes?

The wires in walls join together to make a **circuit**.

A **circuit** means a loop. It has no loose ends. Electricity flows around and around the loop.

A simple **circuit** is made up of a battery pack, a **bulb**, a **bulb holder,** and two wires.

Battery pack

Bulb

Bulb holder

Wires

Join one end of each wire to the battery pack.

Join the other ends to the **bulb holder** and screw in the **bulb**.

Will the bulb light up?

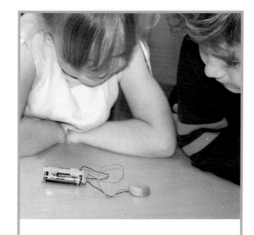

Connect a buzzer to a circuit. The electricity makes it buzz.

• Can you see the loop made by this circuit?
Follow it around with your finger.

What if the bulb does not light?
Perhaps the wires don't touch the
battery, or **connect**. This is a
break in the circuit.

Break

If the wires are attached to the
same ends of the bulb holder,
the bulb is not part of the
loop, or circuit. It won't light!

Do you know how a switch works?

When you press a switch, you make a **break** in the circuit. The bulb goes off.

When you press the switch the other way, the wires **connect** and the bulb goes on!

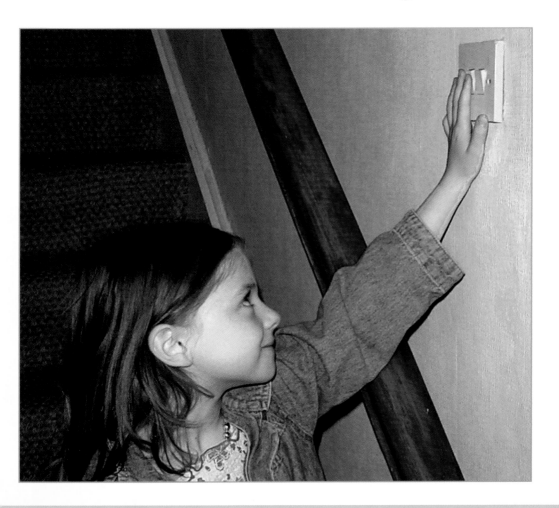

• Can you guess what happens when electric wires are damaged in a storm?

Electricity can also make things move.

Electric **motors** make these toy cars whiz around a track. Can you see the circuits they are connected to?

The train on page 4 has a **motor.** It gets its electricity from the wires above it.

This bus also has an electric **motor.** But it gets its energy from batteries.

The scientific name for a battery is a **cell.** **Cells** give a shuttle energy out in space.

Space shuttle

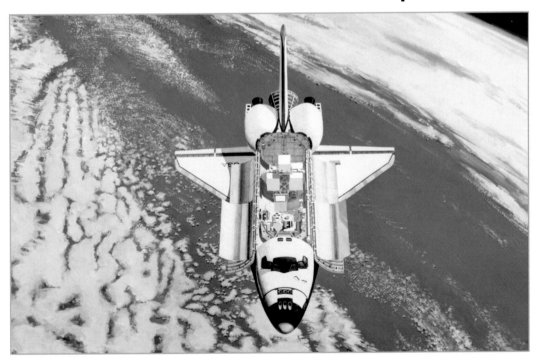

Why do you think a bus or space shuttle can't use a lead?

We make electricity
in different ways.
A **power plant** burns
fuels like coal and oil.

Coal

This machine
looks like a big
fan. When the
wind blows, the
machine spins.

This turns a
turbine, which
makes electricity
when it moves.

22

Storm clouds can make electricity called **lightning.** You see a flash of light.

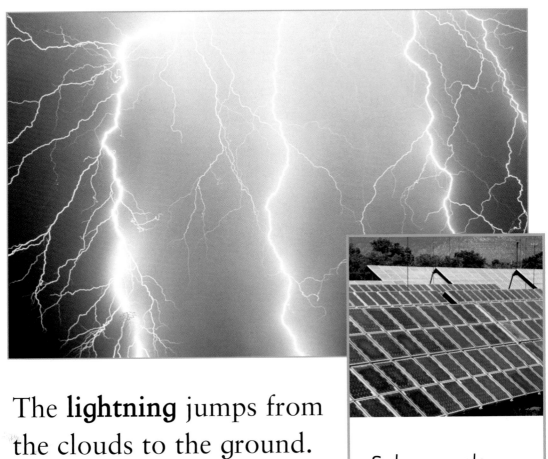

The **lightning** jumps from the clouds to the ground.

Then you hear a rumbling sound. This is thunder!

Solar panels make electricity when the sun shines on them.

• Where in the world would solar panels work best?

POWER CUT!

Look out for words about **electricity**.

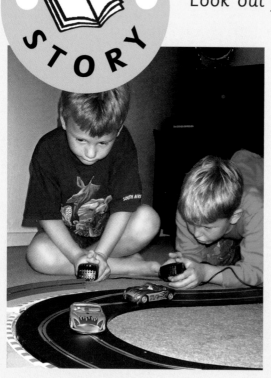

Mom was in the kitchen when the two boys ran in.

"It's raining," said Hugh. "Can we play with our **electric** cars?"

"Dry your hands first," said Mom.

Mom **plugged** the **lead** into the **outlet**. Hugh pressed the **switch**. His car shot off the track!

"It won't work there," said Luke. "The **motor** needs **electricity** from the track to make it go."

Then Uncle Jim came in. "May I borrow that **lead**?" he asked. "The **batteries** have run out in my radio."

"Only if you're quick!" joked Hugh.

"I just want to hear the news," said Uncle Jim.

"There's a storm coming."

"Cool! That means **lightning**," said Hugh.

"Yes," said Uncle Jim. "We should stay **safe** indoors. **Lightning** can be dangerous."

"What if the **lightning** cuts off the power?" asked Luke. "It will be dark soon."

"Here's my flashlight," said Hugh. He **switched** it on. But nothing happened!

"Turn the **batteries** the other way around," said Mom. "Look at the **positive** and **negative** signs."

Still nothing happened!

"Try this new **bulb**," said Uncle Jim.

Luke screwed it in. The flashlight worked!

Thunder rumbled nearby. "Uh-oh," said Hugh.

Suddenly, there was big flash and a loud bang. All the **lights** went off!

Uncle Jim tried the **switch**. "No luck," he said.

"It's a power failure. The **lightning** may have hit the **wires** from the **power plant**."

"The phone is dead, too," said Mom.
"Use your cell phone," said Luke. "It runs on **batteries** and **connects** without a **lead**."

Mom **lit** some candles.
"Don't knock them
over," she said.

"I'm a bit cold now,"
said Luke.
"Is the **heat** on?"

"No. It's **electric**, too," said Mom.
"And so is the stove!"

"Don't worry,"
said Uncle Jim.
"People all over the
world live without
electricity. They use
wood or oil for **heat**
and **light**. So can we!"

Uncle Jim brought
in some wood and
lit the fire.

Luke and Hugh sat next to the fire.
"Not too close," said Uncle Jim.

"We can toast some bread on it too,"
said Mom.

"I'm bored," said Hugh. "Can we watch TV?"
"It's **electric** too, silly," said Luke.

"We don't need **electricity** to play cards,"
said Uncle Jim.
"The winner gets the first piece of toast!"
shouted Hugh.

Suddenly, the **lights** came on.
"Great! The **mains** electricity
must be back on," said Mom.

"Too bad," said Hugh.
"I liked playing in the dark!"

"Me too," said Luke. "But now
I know how much we use **electricity**.
Without power, we wouldn't have TVs, CDs,
or computer games!"

Write a list of **electric** machines that **plug** in
or use **batteries**. Draw pictures of how you
use these **machines** at home or at school.

I switch
on a lamp.

I listen to
my CD
player.

QUIZ

What gives this train **energy**?

Answer on page 5

What does this **safety** sign mean?

Answer on page 12

What do cars use a **battery** for?

Answer on page 14

What do these electric objects do?

Bulb　　**Switch**　　**Battery**

INDEX

B
battery 14
break 18
bulb 16

C
cell 20
circuit 16
connect 18

E
electricity 4
energy 4

F
flow 6

H
heat 10
holder 16

L
lead 8
light 10
lightning 22

M
machine 4
mains 12
motor 20

N
negative 14

O
outlet 8

P
plug 8
positive 14

power plant 22
pylon 6

S
safe 12
shock 12
sound 10
switch 8

T
turbine 22

W
wire 6